WE MAMMALS
IN HOSPITABLE
TIMES

WE MAMMALS
IN HOSPITABLE
TIMES

JYNNE
DILLING
MARTIN

CARNEGIE MELLON UNIVERSITY PRESS
PITTSBURGH 2015

ACKNOWLEDGMENTS

Grateful acknowledgment is made to the editors and readers of the following publications in which many of these poems first appeared: *The Boston Review, Granta, The Kenyon Review, The Literary Review, New England Review, Ploughshares, TriQuarterly*, and *Slate*.

A fellowship from Yaddo and a grant from the National Science Foundation's Antarctic Artists and Writers Program were both a great help in the creation of this book. I am indebted to the kind and generous people I met in both snowbound nirvanas, most especially Ira Sachs, Jesse Finkelstein (by proxy), Peter West, Elaine Hood, Cara Sucher, Jeb Barrett, Breezy Jackson, Paul Koubek, Joolee Aurand, Bill Jirsa, Anne Todgham & co., Michael Deany, and Sheila Corwin.

Book design by Julia Petrich

Library of Congress Control Number 2014943695
ISBN 978-0-88748-596-1

10 9 8 7 6 5 4 3 2

CONTENTS

Because grief unites us,

like the locked antlers of moose

who die on their knees in pairs.

—William Matthews

REASONS TO CONSIDER SETTING OURSELVES ON FIRE

Maybe, pilgrim, if I permit you to sleep on my floor tonight, tomorrow
every house on this block will burn to the ground except mine.

Never mind that we've rocketed beyond the age of miracles, that
snorting herds of swine no longer drown themselves en masse

in Middle Eastern seas, that gone are men in woolen robes riding
immortal white camels, gone too those who knelt before them in dirt.

Gone is the dirt, so holiness must be sought in other fertile crescents.
Tricky, isn't it, when we don't even know what a hairshirt looks like?

Any given window could be a one-way mirror behind which God
sits watching. Any given person cuts a path to a more perfect place.

Undoubtedly the polar bears at the zoo both dream that all other
animals will discover, upon waking, their bodies buried in snow.

SOME IMPORTANT CLARIFICATIONS

Don't get testy. We are all pilgrims since pilgrim means stranger.

A stranger is a stray person or cat wandering without an owner.

Owners are fools. What the hell do you own? Quickly fling it away.

Helvetica is Satan's favorite typeface. He also likes helmets and saying hello.

Greeting cards are an effective way to let a friend in trouble know you care.

"Double trouble" may sound funny, but en garde: things are now twice as bad.

Remember what once seemed catastrophic turned out, after all, to be good.

Good and God are closely related, but bear no ties to goblins or Godiva.

Chocolate must be eaten irrespective of the frownings of dentists.

No doctor has a single lab result explaining where we proceed after earth.

Earth is the third planet from the sun, and its center holds a billion nickels.

APOLOGIA PRO VITA SUA

For years they whispered behind me on the bus. I searched for a stop
but in my condition, all homes looked unfamiliar and all unknowns

the same. People, machines, the stars. I had this wish, as I numbly
scissored out holes in back issues of *National Geographic*—

gams of satiny whales, flanges of baboons, even once a pale paper hive
that held tightly forty thousand digger bees thickly buzzing—to plunge

both my hands into the furred insensate crush. What stopped me then
still stops me now. I cannot risk a trap. My lungs ache from hours hiding

under bathtub water, swallowed soap stinging. Food from cans tastes
strange so I often do not eat it. I remember the cut-out prophets tacked

to blue feltboard at church, how I was told puppets would save me.
Don't you see why I did what I did? I can never be certain that imposters

aren't sitting in for my relatives. Nine of ten times, if you think it, it is true.
The skilled can fool even a talented scientist, his x-rays and sharpened tools.

WHAT BREAKS FIRST

As the iceberg shears off the submarine periscope, the noise
is less groan, more wild animal shriek. "Trust me," said the captain

piloting toward gunfire to see what the Russians are up to these days.
The sea ice resembles a cracked white lung steadily swelling

then sinking as high tide fades away. Already birds and
barnacles and butterflies are shifting their habitats poleward,

the eelgrass and jellyfish will be fine, but the basements
of coastal cities will begin to flood, an inch at a time.

The polar bear at the zoo makes the child start to cry:
why doesn't he move? Animals who cannot acclimate

to shifting conditions engender scientific argument
over what breaks first: the heart or the brain. In the heart

of the Arctic, underwater microphones listen for enemy traffic.
The noise made by a million barnacle larvae swimming north

is less hiss or whisper, more betrayed stare. When rations ran low,
polar explorers ate one less biscuit. When biscuits ran out,

the horses were first to be shot. In another sixty thousand years
the mouth of the Beardmore Glacier will spit out their bones.

THE EFFECTS OF EARTH'S MAGNETIC POLES ON FREE-SPACE PARTICLE FLUX

The whale battles a horned sea monster on the pages of a picture book,
the villain in reindeer mittens paddles a stolen oomiak upriver;

a child's finger traces woodblock prints of the northern lights
made by an Icelandic woman who was last to hear Vatnajökull rumble;

how could I have been last to know, I wrote in my journal twice.
Are cosmic rays the birth cries or death gasps of matter?

inquires the physicist as he reweighs each fallen nucleus;
all efforts are made to trace the lost high-altitude balloon

which leaked gas as it sank, rippling through the Arctic sky;
the sled dog who breaks through a crevasse pulls all the rest down.

The poison in a polar bear liver made the explorer blister and turn blue,
how his skin peeled snakelike head to foot will long be retold;

the bride in scarlet boots and a beaded collar is soon forgotten,
kneeling pregnant in sealskin trousers as she heats the hoosh;

she last saw her husband as a vanishing dot on the horizon.
The Eskimo language is often consulted by crossword makers,

kayak, mukluk, igloo, ukluk penciled in by the lawyer on a train;
the newborn screams and the mother's blood spreads on the snow,

the sun never dips past seventy degrees, and the volcano glow reddens;
there is a thirst that is unquenchable, no matter how much snow you melt.

Are you all well, sounds the megaphone from the bridge of the ship,
but no answer is made from the hut and they see no signs of life;

the chapter concludes with the sea monster spearing the whale's flank,
for life is a scattershot business, and why pretend it is anything else;

the direction and changing colors of the aurora cannot be foretold.

REPERCUSSIONS OF THE CURRENT IMPORT/EXPORT RATIO

They smuggled turnip seeds into the new world by
sewing them in a hem. Welcome, the customs official said.

There is a mystery about people when they leave us:
how does a skipped stone pick the moment to sink?

A donkey drags a plow through the dirt. Later in life
at the circus he will learn to do mathematics with his hoof,

stomp out answers to questions of addition and subtraction,
astonish crowds with his understanding of these problems.

I draw images of who I used to be and drown them in the lake;
I bind them to rocks to prevent them from ever resurfacing.

The customs official sinks crates of contraband into the sea
and wonders where each bullet might have been bound;

the fireworks he hides and explodes the following summer,
his face becoming the strangest colors beneath the bursts.

The snake crawling out of her skin pulls it inside out
like a nylon stocking: I wonder who would recognize me now.

Sometimes seeds lodge deep in clothing and years later sprout
out of gravesites and dresser drawers, turnips for lunch,

turnips for soups, turnips for dinner. I asked the donkey
the odds you'll ever come back. I waited for his leg to lift.

RESISTANCE MOVEMENTS THROUGHOUT HISTORY

Evacuation procedures prioritize the rescue of larger animals;
smaller zoo mammals are rumored to be left behind in fires.

Wailing and trapped: the way you came is the way you will go.
Lichen form tufts to resist the pressure of arctic snow

but no finger can stop the groundwater and its relentless swell,
mole rats gasping upwards for air, the gag of liquid in lung.

Platoons of ants interlock legs to form floating balls
of panicked bodies. The child who sees another child fall, cries.

But who will look after the nocturnal bumblebee bat,
when firemen tap at his glass and move on, thinking no one home?

I wonder each day who will save me, and if it's a question
for a deity or city government. "Dear councilperson," I begin.

"Upholstered chairs seem luxurious, but lay traps for the health."
I press my ear to the mattress and listen for a telltale click.

Lichen compose the bulk of the caribou diet: stooping, they sniff it
hiding under snow and gouge out craters with a sharp front hoof.

The way of the world is attack by surprise: the bear hovers
behind the hive, the next door neighbors are named as spies.

A cocooned moth tugs open a tiny hole. Sometimes I mix up fear
with hissed instructions. As another silk thread snaps, whispers rise.

THE RIVER WHOSE SOURCE LIES BEYOND THIS MAP

Wood is stacked on all sides of my house and set ablaze.
To what end! I cry as the walls collapse in reply.

Each morning I insist my neighbors guess what I dreamt:

instead of a human head, a malformed fish mouthing a message?
The slow morse of landing strip lights? A doctor departing unmasked?

Some hours I keep a detailed score: it can be so boring here at times.
At others I pretend to care, unsure if the difficulty is theirs or mine.

I read books to learn the meaning of these signs:

one alleges my body walled in alabaster means self-annihilation,
another that a pen of pigs tells the number of holes in my skull.

Tonight I buried a bull but left a single horn protruding from the dirt.

NOISE PUTS PRESSURE ON THE BRAIN

The cat licking its fur the wrong direction bodes ill:
suddenly you have a foreign body lodged in your throat.

I could tell you the story of the beggar and the bone;
you would not respond, pretend to be hard of hearing.

Millions went hungry while the wealthy used vats of flour
to whiten their wigs, white as dough, whiter than doves.

Once we were thick as birds wing to wing in a nest,
hearts the size of thumbs tapping together, same song each day.

Now a rasping, the only sound, from gardeners sweeping
the empty lawn with enormous brooms: does one die

from such a silence? A beggar once heated a cutlet
over a fire and the fire burned up the meat. Greedy fire!

he cried and doused it with his cup of water. That night
he died of thirst and cold. I heard you choking but I

pretended to be asleep. Maggots slipped through the twigs,
fell onto grass uneaten. So plump. The whitest we'd ever seen.

LONELY WE WERE THOUGH NEVER LEFT ALONE

I can no longer mix with other people. The tiger grows gradually larger
as he steals along the trail. It sounds like a riddle but I will explain:

after a flood the ditch remains, the river derailed still gnaws
at the floors of cement basements. My own abysses deepen every day.

As I sleep, your ghost slides in through my slackened mouth, I dream
of our youthful fucking, our softness, how in ancient times we had tails.

The earth is falling in a pin-straight line: it is time that curves around us,
we are doomed to orbit back into the maw of our mistakes,

discover the same hairs on bedsheets, false hairs of various colors,
I thought you said it would be the last time that this happened.

We learn of our crimes from our dreams: I find you dead but don't know
what to do. The tiger, ready to roar, will not stop walking toward me.

IN WHICH OUR HEROINE IS COAXED OUT OF HER SHELL

Ask and I will give the nations to you, you who have not known to ask—

an abacus bead slid so long in one dimension you thought
there was only this: to figure in the calculations of others,

to be thumbed on the margins of inscrutable quadratic equations.
Not to be the frogman with a harpoon descending deep,
not his fogged mask, his oiled suit, or his slippery-scaled prey

eeling in the murk as he holds his breath, lifts and takes aim—

merely the one who studied his hunt in a picture book,
illustrated princes strangling dragons put back on a long-ago shelf.

You always confused why and how you failed. You mixed up
strangers and relatives, mistook wallpaper patterns for stains,
brochures for colorful journeys, persons clouded in smoke for saints.

To know what it is to slay and be slain, and how there is no difference—

then you will not fear your desires, then I can give you the nations,
their flags, their legislatures and municipal towers, their sewers and snow,

their arbitrary borders, the brigades patrolling them noon and night,
pistol barrels slowly wiped with cloths, every bullet that will and will not
be fired, I can give you the lungs of every creature tautening with air,

how they deflate over and over and over and without sorrow.

IN WHICH A KINDLY DOCENT GUIDES ME THROUGH THIS WORLD

Without him I'd have never seen by the highway a deer courageously
eating weeds, or narrow closets with rows of metal hangers,

how all day the tensed wires get sealed in the dark,
or learned not to stare at the sun or at old men collapsing,

how to grip with a potholder the roughest pineapple.
I like how he rests his hand on my head as we walk

through gymnasiums with their inflated rubber balls
and a strong sad smell he calls chalk, and hallways, which are

rooms where no one lives, and peopled rooms where fabric pulls
shut to hide the sky. When I feel flushed from all this,

he takes a lettuce leaf from the cooler and presses
its firm green ribbing to my forehead, but still I lie awake,

cataloging the disparate events he marks by years: celebrations,
invasions, a measurement of sun. So much to still understand.

THE FIRST OF THREE ATTEMPTS TO UNDERSTAND OUR NEIGHBORS

The northern lands fascinate and puzzle the rest of the world.
Are bells removed from reindeer before their meat is served?

Who's Who? is a good source of information about the elite
though it omits what they store in their freezers.

The government keeps tabs on incomes and individuals
and answers queries with glossy photos of our leader.

A well-bred person grasps the truth without being told;
parked cars prevent the rest of us from seeing it coming.

The definition of good breeding has been revised
to eliminate the falcon tethered to a leather-gloved fist.

Our ancestors can now be traced past the clustered continents
to a single grasping antenna fossilized in chalk.

In military parlance, retirement means withdrawal.
Rabbits are souvenirs. To shave is to speak out of turn.

Mafia men laugh at full volume if they suspect a wiretap.
The silence of a dying patient is hard on the hospital staff.

Still others we simply have no explanation for,
like the ones who enter and exit through chimneys,

or who can reach into a horse and yank it inside out.
Who have such sharp teeth. Who leave us and never look back.

CASE IN POINT: BOLOGNA

Microwave bologna:
it swells into a shiny pink hill.
Most things would just die.

AND PERSONS AND ITS HABITS AND ITS PAST

They do not mean to behave so. They are easily stumped. They rarely speak.
Can you guess what they are thinking? No, for if asked, they might say,
a flecked brown egg. They might say, estrangement, and leave it at that.

Their sleep is a restless sleep, for they do not know what we know.
They pronounce danger as dagger, have a weakness for the past tense,
though seem lovely at times, when at the seaside, or rinsing hair.

Sometimes they take each other's pulse with a strap and a machine,
sometimes with their own pinched thumbs. Now they feel normal.
Now they feel nervous. Impossible, really, to settle on which one . . .

These are just a few examples. We recorded others. The more cages
the better! And then they put bodies under rocks. Nevertheless we did once
tape them on all fours engaging in what might could be termed a kindness.

PROTECTIVE MEASURES WILL PREVENT COSTLY DISASTERS

I blackened the loops of each word in the letters
you posted, trying in vain to find traces of fraud.

That was discouraging. The doctors politely masked their laughter
but it would be madness to suppose they were innocents in the plot.

The animals act as if they sleep at night but the wolf yard is not secure.
Next door hens collapse in fits of nerves, dander thickening the air.

Tigers pace beneath trellised steel, over which decorative vines
are trained: subduing defiance is the role of ornamental shrubbery.

Or is it to obscure danger? The dinner gong smothers
shots in the basement, metal forks pulsing as we eat our peas.

The risks of a sudden move are revealed by its fruits. The significance
of fruit is signaled by their colorful skins: what else is an apple

if not a terrible warning? I draw deep on my sense of mistrust.
I've warned you not to wait for the hunter before you hide

and I've alluded to the inadequacy of the antelope house
a dozen times in previous missives. You make me spell things out.

RESOLUTIONS

When the urge to look under a plastic tarp overcomes me,
to cut off my hand.

To ignore concerns for safety, despite noises
coming from your toolshed.

On the day of the second-prize carnival rabbit, to say
I do not keep score, though that will be a lie.

As beloved objects begin to disappear, to bake
cakes molded in their shape.

During wolverine weather, to cloak against snow, and move
swiftly on all fours.

The night I am captured, tortured, and biting a stick,
to taste its hard green tang.

When I wake from the dream where you sew my eyelids shut,
to keep them closed all that day.

Each time the assembled bread on our table resembles a tower, to repeat:
it is bread, it is bread, it is not a tower.

When an owl alights on my hand and you scream,
to make note of your reaction.

CASE IN POINT: CATS

Our cat hates vacuums.
We laugh as he runs and hides.
Silly cat. Scared to die.

IN WHICH OUR HEROINE CONSIDERS HER ALTERNATIVES

Draw any beast by starting with a circle! Then pencil in tusks
or distended bowels or a sweater-vest with scratchy argyle diamonds . . .

Naturally complications accrue with each additional triangle tooth,
each subsequent month of discarded girlfriends and gods and gas masks,
years of scribbled decisions and enemy blood clumping on our fur.

Our beginnings never know our ends: every day I start knitting a skull
and have yet to bind off a one. Umpteen distinguished civil servants devote

box after box of chalk to population patterns and projections,
and still I overheard the chief comptroller in the bathroom stall saying,
"Are these ideas right or wrong?" as he peed his morning coffee away.

So I subscribed to *Understanding Your Worm*. O simplest of ovoids, never
have you slammed the phone or weepingly packed an overnight bag!

I confess that personal ad in the March issue was mine: ISO ascetic male
who loves long walks through leaves, who like me, spirals when disturbed.
It stung, yes, to get no replies. Postage perhaps was out of reach. But at last

out back I found love nibbling the pink guts of a squirrel. Such equanimity
as his nose pressed death! How did it end, you ask? Reader, I married him.

AUTOPSIES WERE MADE WITH THE FOLLOWING RESULTS

I draw uncounted fugues from pianos but no consolation,
and recall the ogre who mistook hot coals for roasted nuts,

and dream of riding atop my sadness like it is a horse.
My horse may be black yet in darkness is easily mounted,

and the coals may have long collapsed into ash, but the burn
on the tongue remains. The children dance, the children sing:

touch teeth, touch leather, can't have back for ever and ever.
Just as a spun knife on a table will tell the future,

the thickness of anyone's ice will predict the past.
"You owe me an explanation!" I shout at the vanishing man,

and though I can disturb the quiet of the jungle with my cries,
I cannot force a fly to rip off its wings. I would like to strip you

naked and suspend you in a net, exposed to insect stings,
I would like to suck in your last exhale as you expire,

I wish we could begin again. Touch white, swap back if I like.
Just as a man of faith can carry off the ocean in a simple shell,

the fatalist who opens the piano lid must play on.
The oyster will not be sated until filled with pearl.

OUR HEROINE IS STALKED BY A WHITE ARCTIC FOX

Its wet breath wheezes between the trees.
Some days she sees it skulking on the horizon,

or is that just sun witching his windows,
white furred flicker?

With thickest glasses, through fuliginous air,
she makes out figures penciled roughly

on a sanatorium chart: an eyeball, strappados,
garrote, elongated jaw of fangs. As she runs,

a sinking feeling down another drainage tunnel.
One by one, her neighbor's teeth get stolen away.

Five wayward years in the desert of Lop,
still one dusk among crackled mollusk shells

slender prints dented the yellow clay.
Her final resort is fasting, flogging, phlebotomy,

blood fleamed from her side and drained
quart by quart into a white enamel bowl.

A multitude of crows alighted on her house
such as no one imagined existed those days.

A SPELL FOR GOING SAFELY FORTH BY DAY

The hunter pushes a bullet beneath his tongue to fix his aim,
or is it to stave off thirst? The antelope pausing at the brook

fears each snap. The child drinks, the child is tired, for the child
the day is done. Some animals enter caves and never reemerge:

only later, studying footprints, did I realize I'd seen you dying.
I knew nothing of how things perish, how the feet falter first,

doctors nudge tubes down throats, the last word might be hello.
I see planes fly by but not the pilots' faces. I see a bicycle just abandoned:

a crime? My mind replays the upturned wheel's dwindling spin.
Thirst drives sailors to drench their clothes in seawater, and relief

drives the riderless horse to run, two arrows askew in her saddle.
Later she will stagger; later shots, man overboard, mutiny.

But now only the shock of water, cold on the antelope's tongue.
All is still. You are coasting down a hill. There is nothing here to fear.

THE FADS AND FASHIONS OF OUR LIFE AND TIMES

The dancer's dying words: get my swan costume ready.
No one stirs from her bed. Elsewhere a hollowed pharaoh

lies with fingers and toes capped in golden thimbles
as a sandstorm thickens outside. A human-headed bird

evacuates his body by day and at night returns to nest
in his emptied stomach. The purpose of mummification

is to make a good first impression: even kings are anxious
when entering a crowded room. The dancer recalls

how blood drained from her lifted arms in the darkness
while she waited for the next curtain to rise, how vital

it seemed to smile. In the din of the after party it's hard
to hear: does she dislike the hyacinth or the asylum?

Harder and harder to say what will win over the rest;
like the barbarians who did not know how to feint

or retreat, some plow headlong into foreign fields
setting everyone behind them on fire. Others prepare

carefully for the year with poultices and prayer,
thinking that will stave off demonic occupation. But

someday an invading army will seize each of our homes.
They will not understand our language, no, nor us them.

CASE IN POINT: PROTOZOA

In biology, I slept through the film.
Protozoa swam from cell to cell to cell.
I hope they never need my help.

POP QUIZ ON ALL YOU'VE LEARNED SO FAR

Who first sketched a human appendix?

Which of these have you seen so far: an abacus, geologist, chum, a parrot's perch.

If you chose a parrot's perch, where did you hide that parrot?

Sorcerers, circle one: too common, common, not common enough.

When did the first giraffe arrive at Shun-Chi's court?

His tail rubbed out his tracks: yes or no.

How did you harm so-and-so, and why?

Fortunately death, true or false.

Do the billions of stars we can and cannot see contain so many habitable worlds?

When cadaver dissections began in the 1300s surgeons would first cut open
the_____ .

Do horses on land logically dictate that there also be horses in seas?

Better to wager on the leaper, or the one asleep in its nest?

In what calendar year did the sum total of the dead exceed the number yet to live?

Define reincarnation without using the word body. Remember to be brief.

HOW LONG IS THE COAST OF BRITAIN?

Eels loop frantic in buckets of blood,
the log aflame cracks as it collapses to ash,

but the shot doe slackens in silence.
It is the hour for farewells. It is the hour

for suckling the stray, for swaddling the runt,
a last chance to smooth back your hair.

Later the polar seas too will capitulate,
swiftly entombing the planet, gravity will dwindle,

the moon unbridled will glide out of sight.
I can watch in slow motion an arrow's flight,

I can blame the unseen archer for every wound,
but I cannot prevent an adopted parrot

from shrieking unfamiliar names.
What about you will I forget first, and second,

one minute splits into how many moments,
what do the thousand eyes of a housefly see?

Each man will die at the rate he feels inclined.
Every measured pebble adds an inch.

WHEN I THINK OF WHAT THE FUTURE MUST BRING

There will be no vegetables with dimpled skin, no onions at all,
no lumpy tubers with bulbous names, turnip, yam, rutabaga, beet!

All food will come in shades of apricot, snow, and viridian green,
you will have a new satin robe and sable slippers with pearl beads,

armfuls of leaves, twenty white falcons who will pivot at your bidding,
a faucet that will gush on a whim the sparkling drink of your choice,

a rare glass paperweight collection, a cat who, like you, will never die.
Will old friends and lovers be waiting for you there? I do not know.

Would you really want that anyhow? Why not let this planet
and its people spin away. Choose to remember them faintly

and without affection, as characters from a supermarket paperback,
the footing but not the feeling of a dance you once performed.

You'll amuse yourself by conjuring storms on Saturn and her
thirty moons, then visiting each, ice-nipped, numb, nude, free.

OUT OF WHOSE WOMB CAME THE ICE?

The Yup'ik Eskimo believes the crusted earth is perched
on a turtle shell; the vulcanologist peering over the cone

sees the veins of her primordial eye as she blinks back.
The geologist drills down toward wrinkled skin, forgetting

what his ancestors knew: the longer you dig into darkness,
the harder it will be to know your own face in a mirror.

The greater the pressure of pack ice enveloping Shackleton's ship
the louder the officer in the crow's nest recited the book of Job:

The hoary frost of heaven, who hath gendered it?
Unfortunately Mrs. Chippy, the carpenter's cat, must be shot,

wrote Ernest in his journal. A snow petrel attempted a dive
and the ice closed on her forever. The carpenter closed his eyes

at the crack of the gun. *The waters are hid as with a stone.*
An unexplained virus is decimating reptile populations,

bats mottled in fungus pile up at the mouths of caves,
instruments lowered on strings cannot find an answer.

An underwater camera in the sludge of an Antarctic lake
shows a carpet of cyanobacteria radiating orange light.

Maybe life on Earth started like this, or maybe this is the end.
When Yup'ik girls have their period, they know not to look at the sky.

WE CAN EAT ONLY MARSHMALLOWS AND STILL SURVIVE

Scientists, scientists, they fill our heads with lies!

Clouds composed of water droplets? Friend, they are swarms of albino locust.
     Listen at dawn for their chirr.

Lightning is generated by severed power lines lashing the plains.

Stars, the fiery coals of hand-rolled cigarettes smoked by lonely astronauts in orbit.

A U-shaped magnet entombed in Utah prevents our moon from floating away.

Gravity? Bollocks. The despair of all the animals weighs us down.

The millimeter, they made it up!

They keep the oldest man alive locked in an Albany lab. How he loved his pet
     brontosaurus, her flowing lavender mane . . .

It's possible to forgive and forget: successful trial runs have been done with mice.

And it's not angular momentum that keeps earth spinning—it's all the zebras
     with sharp black hooves running, running, running.

A CRANE HANGS LIKE AN ICICLE

The citizen consulting the charts
feels vexed; that which we call Mars
is not a planet, no planet

can hopscotch backwards and forwards
across the sky. No letter
written in a state of insanity

can be punished as an offense.
When I try to imagine my life to come
I see a lump of sea glass buried,

ground to a blinding clarity under
centuries of sand. Perhaps within our gymnasia
cattle will graze, a capful of vinegar

will revive the cricket after the drought.
He will teach us to unlock and spring,
the trick of bending deeply back.

We can only describe what gravity
is not like, it is not intermittent like birds
spaced on a wire, it cannot be slit open

like the venous lining of a songbird stomach,
it does not chee-chaw like their song.
Is it gravity that prevents us from knowing

our future? Or is it a secret pact
binding us to past generations, we call it
withholding, they call it love.

ON A BUS FROM MALL TO MALL IN VERY HEAVY RAIN

One day with closed eyes you'll play on a rosewood piano
in a dove gray kimono, satin rustling over the pedals.

In your pockets, nickels and quarters will be perfectly round,
arithmetic will come easy, as will breath and tennis and sleep.

At your door, a line of cats with combed white fur
to serve you that day on a domed glass platter.

The ice cream topping your frosted, flower-trimmed
yellow butter cake will change flavor with every lick,

the sky sliding by, a shade of silver only you can see.
Deer will gather at hedges to lap sea salt from your palm.

The thunderheads will split to reveal seven suns,
six burning just for you.

IT WAS HUSHED UP FOR REASONS WE CANNOT EXPLAIN

We watched them through special glasses: we saw but could not hear
how they removed their clothes and bathed in a lake or a narrow tiled stall,
gave affection easily, pulled skins off fruit, remained indoors during darkness.

We did not want their money and we intended them no harm.
It was a novelty, that's all, their spatulas and envy, their assassinations,
how they employed unleashed dogs to flush game birds from thickets.

We pulled their planet closer. We made programs on their primitive ways.
Charming, how they ride atop animals, the location and depth of their graves!
Moreover we laughed and laughed at how many of them ate basil.

We once sent one to walk among them but they terribly misunderstood.
Oh, we regret that error. We'd seen before how they fork snails out of shells,
wall convicts in caves, but still, the outcome was unexpected.

We have agreed that though they enchant us, they are not reliable
for our purposes. We must let them go. We wish we could tell them goodbye
as they do one another, with hands or telephones, though sometimes not at all.

AM GOING SOUTH, AMUNDSEN

An oil painting of a jaguar eating an emperor penguin
is the start of a daydream in the Royal Society library.

Nineteen ponies wedged in narrow wooden stalls
sail south; they will soon go blind from miles of radiant snow,

lap at volcanic ash for a last smack of salt, be shot
and fed to dogs. For now they sway this way, sway that.

The magnetic needle dips. Only afterwards we ask if it cost
too much. Will this species be here tomorrow or not?

says the scientist to her assembled team. The ponies eat oats
in silence, the instruments keep ticking, the icy water

washes on and off the deck. A bell abruptly rings a warning:
oxidative stress, methane concentrations, too much heat.

The dragonfish lays her pearlescent eggs beneath the ice
and for ten months stands guard. The sea stars sway this way,

sway that. We all hope for the best. The adaptive might survive,
the needy will not. Then again, the adaptive likely won't either.

Sorry we realized too late: we wipe reindeer hair from our eyes,
the glaciated passages too dazzling to quite see clearly.

REVELATIONS

Like an adopted cat, your planet hates its name.

Your entreaties bore it and turning, it declines to respond.
Oh you try flattery, this compliment or that:

you study its seasons and tricks, replicate ice with machines.

You have given it roads and a seven-paged encyclopedia entry,
molded globes in its image, spangled its moon with flags,

all while plotting your jailbreak. Don't think it doesn't sense that,

and if it does, no wonder the snow hangs tightly in the sky
ready on moment's notice to bury the building where you sit

sketching a future world of telepathy, golden eggs, fire.

Boys, the afterlife will be a pie of live bird heads.
Their song so cracked you won't dare take a bite.

CASE IN POINT: CROWS

The crows sat down.
"It's finally time," their President said.
Nothing ends as we expect.

LIFE MAY HAVE BEGUN MORE THAN ONCE

The spacecraft will exit the magnetosphere tomorrow;
the Soviet polar expedition is allotted a bimonthly bath.

Years before, an explorer halfway into *A Broken Promise*
abandoned the dog-eared novel in his reindeer skin sack.

Up north, herds of reindeer shake off snow and lift
antlered heads as a pinprick of light dissolves in the sky;

Dmitri Klimov emerges wrinkled, pink and howling,
numb from his icy dive. Back then you knew nothing:

now you know how to begin again. The geologist
kneeling on barren nunatak stuffs a briefcase full

of Antarctic fossils: insects, pollen grains, roots, and fronds.
Meteorites are thought to have obliterated life

at least twice before our turn arrived. The seal is born
with her permanent teeth erupting from soft pink gums;

soon she'll gnaw holes in sheets of unbroken ice.
How soon after birth will you first go into the water?

whispers the marine biologist; in sunlight the silver lanugo
of the small pup shines white. *Exi abeo immunde spiritus,*

sang the priest as he baptized the child. Be here now,
chants Ram Dass in the headphones of the astronaut,

who takes a bite of dehydrated apple, flips a switch,
floats weightless to a window to watch our planet pass by.

ALWAYS THROW THE FIRST FISH BACK

The world resembles a phantom vessel destined
to sail but never reach port. The kidnapping victim

bound to a sawmill tries to loosen the ropes in vain
as electric sparks shower down, unsure if help is on the way.

Later in life he will apprentice with a sailor and learn
to pull apart every knot. I am not afraid of shackles

but dread the traps that precede them: the decoy duck,
the pitfall, the plainclothes officer posing as a friend.

Once imprisoned you can relax into your chains,
befriend the rats who will elect you mayor,

you will have time to entertain their many complaints,
to feel the stones beneath you separately, round or pointed,

to chalk mark each day, but the difficult trick is to die
without thinking of betrayal, the quicksand under the bed.

If you can learn not to see all nets as snares, you can stroll
freely about the ship deck and say, this is the silver mist

hemming us in, there is the anchor ready to drop,
these are the rats who will flee if they sense we are sinking.

DROPPED THINGS ARE BOUND TO SINK

Under the smallest bent-back cricket leg rotates this enormous planet
attesting to a cosmic order, surface washed in light supposed to heal

all wicked men: paralytics, lepers, those whose mouths are packed
with pebbles, blind crows instead of stomachs, telltale signs of shame.

In a field, a black hood over my head, I stood and waited for these rays
to shine inside. Is this faith, how by and by, darkness begins to look like light?

Prophets with soft hair carry fistfuls of crystallized dates and figs, coax
cornstalks out of feces, sound from unstruck cymbals, fur through naked skin.

But the pillars of great temples stand far apart. A lost wind slithers between.
Those who cherish doubt are reborn as salt and carried swiftly shoreward,

taken by tides to an island no one has bothered to name. There I wandered
for many years, gorging on honeycomb, holding myself as I slept.

Why disbelieve all those promises? Answers arrive in trifling waves
or do not come at all. Now I sit on a rock with my back to the wreck and refuse

to turn around. Beneath a hot sun that offers nothing I do not already own,
I suck the meat off a great seabird, kick sand over his crooked bones.

LUMINESCENCE

What is how long it took us to get here
compared to sea turtles exhaling
and inhaling but three times each day,

or the bone hooks of Eskimos
lowered through holes carved in Arctic ice,
spinning down, down, down into the dark.

For years I carried the pelts of past loves
hammered to my chest like birds of prey
nailed to a hunter's wooden gate.

You searched the jagged movements of stars
for signs of another fire as volatile and strong.
Centuries back, the first guillotine blade

was tested on a runaway sheep.
Nowadays so few die of loneliness
we've forgotten we share the disease.

The harder I yanked the nails, the darker
the blood on my hands. Animals continue
to squeeze under splintered fences

but once free in the woods, as night falls
they curl into the lap of an imaginary lost boy.
Stop searching. Close your eyes. The dream remains.

Yellow grease fills the abdomen of the glowworm,
millions swaying on threads in unseen caves.
A new season of fire has begun.

WHAT ENDURES AND WHAT DOES NOT?

Soon this ship will be crushed in a polar storm; below deck,
pages of the *Encyclopedia Britannica* are read aloud,

shredded and used to light pipes. A century later
the preservationist draining antique food tins

sneaks a taste of raspberry jam. That night he'll dream
he digs out a tomb on a glacier filled with bay leaves

still fragrant and green. The emperor penguin egg
tucked warm in the explorer's pocket is delivered intact

to the receptionist desk at the Royal Geographic Society;
the robbery victim nestles a stone between his feet

and rocks back and forth at the bottom of the world.
Enough seal blubber can keep a single lamp burning

for a thousand years; enough knowledge exists to fill
twenty thousand encyclopedia pages. Lost friends

return to us in dreams, but come morning we can't recall
what they wanted. *Snakes, Snell's law, Snowblind*

curl up into hazy tobacco smoke. The amphipods
in test tubes begin to faint from next century's

simulated heat; falling leaves fill the air of our dreams.
The biologist drills a hole in the sea snail's shell

and slides a miniature stethoscope inside, listens
for the heartbeat: it's beating, still beating, still beating.

EVERYTHING WE CAN SEE IN THE UNIVERSE GLOWS

A giant ice cube at South Pole Station captures
extragalactic neutrinos. Please take me to where you are,

pleaded the pregnant Korean widow to her lost love
in a sixteenth-century letter an archaeologist

found folded in a tomb. Telescopes see only light;
faces from our dreams, unspoken desires, dead stars

go undetected. Come to me secretly and show yourself,
she whispered. Hans Spemann plucked a fine hair

from his newborn daughter to tie an embryo egg in half.
The microscope zooms in on a freshly formed eyeball

gazing expectantly back. The archaeologist feels ill,
presses twice-boiled tea leaves to his forehead,

unfolds and refolds the letter again. The fastest thing
in the universe is light; the slowest is forgiving

then forgetting. The seal gnaws a hole in the sea ice,
sunlight flashes on a million emerald cod flitting below.

Captured neutrinos flare pale blue; embryos float
in drops of glistening saline fluid and await their fate.

Quartz cuvettes filled with seawater and lavender dye
slide into a spectrometer, colors the human eye

cannot see fan out inside a box. Please, come in a dream,
there is no limit to what I want to know. I wait here.

NOTES

REASONS TO CONSIDER SETTING OURSELVES ON FIRE was inspired by a *New York Post* photograph of the Central Park Zoo polar bears after a snowstorm.

WHAT BREAKS FIRST quotes a submarine pilot I met in Antarctica.

THE EFFECTS OF EARTH'S MAGNETIC POLES ON FREE-SPACE PARTICLE FLUX includes a cry made by Ernest Shackleton from the bow of *The Endurance*.

REPERCUSSIONS OF THE CURRENT IMPORT/EXPORT RATIO alludes to Robert Bresson's refusal to use a trained donkey in *Au Hasard Balthazar*.

IN WHICH OUR HEROINE IS COAXED OUT OF HER SHELL is for Justin and Erin, with gratitude.

PROTECTIVE MEASURES WILL PREVENT COSTLY DISASTERS cites the 1909 *Annual Report to the Smithsonian* and takes its title from a fortune cookie fortune, as do several other poems in this collection.

IN WHICH OUR HEROINE CONSIDERS HER ALTERNATIVES is dedicated to the one and only Scansion Crew: Adam, Rachel, and Tom.

A SPELL FOR GOING SAFELY FORTH BY DAY takes its title from the Egyptian *Book of the Dead*.

HOW LONG IS THE COAST OF BRITAIN? is for Diana Colbert. We love you.

OUT OF WHOSE WOMB CAME THE ICE? is inspired by the Yup'ik Eskimo stories shared with me by Joolee Aurand, and takes its title from the Book of Job.

ON A BUS FROM MALL TO MALL IN VERY HEAVY RAIN is for my nephews Dove, Zane, and Sequoia.

AM GOING SOUTH, AMUNDSEN is the telegram sent by Roald Amundsen to Robert Falcon Scott in 1910. The poem itself quotes biologist Anne Todgham.

LIFE MAY HAVE BEGUN MORE THAN ONCE is not entirely accurate. The explorer left *A Broken Promise* on a side table in Antarctica where it still sits today, not in his sleeping sack.

DROPPED THINGS ARE BOUND TO SINK takes its title from Marianne Moore's poem "A Graveyard."

LUMINESCENCE is, with all my heart, for Louie.

WHAT ENDURES AND WHAT DOES NOT? includes a biologist drilling a sea snail shell, based on the real life invertebrate work of Amanda Kelley.

EVERYTHING WE CAN SEE IN THE UNIVERSE GLOWS quotes an actual love letter found in 2013 in an ancient Korean tomb.

Previous titles in the Carnegie Mellon Poetry Series

2001

Day Moon, Jon Anderson
The Origin of Green, T. Alan Broughton
Lovers in the Used World, Gillian Conoley
Quarters, James Harms
Mastodon, 80% Complete, Jonathan Johnson
The Deepest Part of the River, Mekeel McBride
Earthly, Michael McFee
Ten Thousand Good Mornings, James Reiss
The World's Last Night, Margot Schilpp
Sex Lives of the Poor and Obscure, David Schloss
Glacier Wine, Maura Stanton
Voyages in English, Dara Wier

2002

Keeping Time, Suzanne Cleary
Astronaut, Brian Henry
What It Wasn't, Laura Kasischke
Slow Risen Among the Smoke Trees, Elizabeth Kirschner
The Finger Bone, Kevin Prufer
Among the Musk Ox People, Mary Ruefle
The Late World, Arthur Smith

2003

Trouble, Mary Baine Campbell
A Place Made of Starlight, Peter Cooley
Taking Down the Angel, Jeff Friedman
Lives of Water, John Hoppenthaler
Imitation of Life, Allison Joseph
Except for One Obscene Brushstroke, Dzvinia Orlowsky
The Mastery Impulse, Ricardo Pau-Llosa
Casino of the Sun, Jerry Williams

2004

The Women Who Loved Elvis All Their Lives, Fleda Brown
The Chronic Liar Buys a Canary, Elizabeth Edwards

Freeways and Aqueducts, James Harms
Prague Winter, Richard Katrovas
Trains in Winter, Jay Meek
Tristimania, Mary Ruefle
Venus Examines Her Breast, Maureen Seaton
Various Orbits, Thom Ward

2005

Things I Can't Tell You, Michael Dennis Browne
Bent to the Earth, Blas Manuel De Luna
Blindsight, Carol Hamilton
Fallen from a Chariot, Kevin Prufer
Needlegrass, Dennis Sampson
Laws of My Nature, Margot Schilpp
Sleeping Woman, Herbert Scott
Renovation, Jeffrey Thomson

2006

Burn the Field, Amy Beeder
The Sadness of Others, Hayan Charara
A Grammar to Waking, Nancy Eimers
Dog Star Delicatessen: New and Selected Poems 1979–2006, Mekeel
    McBride
Shinemaster, Michael McFee
Eastern Mountain Time, Joyce Peseroff
Dragging the Lake, Robert Thomas

2007

Trick Pear, Suzanne Cleary
So I Will Till the Ground, Gregory Djanikian
Black Threads, Jeff Friedman
Drift and Pulse, Kathleen Halme
The Playhouse Near Dark, Elizabeth Holmes
On the Vanishing of Large Creatures, Susan Hutton
One Season Behind, Sarah Rosenblatt
Indeed I Was Pleased with the World, Mary Ruefle
The Situation, John Skoyles

2008

The Grace of Necessity, Samuel Green
After West, James Harms
Anticipate the Coming Reservoir, John Hoppenthaler
Convertible Night, Flurry of Stones, Dzvinia Orlowsky
Parable Hunter, Ricardo Pau-Llosa
The Book of Sleep, Eleanor Stanford

2009

Divine Margins, Peter Cooley
Cultural Studies, Kevin A. González
Dear Apocalypse, K. A. Hays
Warhol-o-rama, Peter Oresick
Cave of the Yellow Volkswagen, Maureen Seaton
Group Portrait from Hell, David Schloss
Birdwatching in Wartime, Jeffrey Thomson

2010

The Diminishing House, Nicky Beer
A World Remembered, T. Alan Broughton
Say Sand, Daniel Coudriet
Knock Knock, Heather Hartley
In the Land We Imagined Ourselves, Jonathan Johnson
Selected Early Poems: 1958-1983, Greg Kuzma
The Other Life: Selected Poems, Herbert Scott
Admission, Jerry Williams

2011

Having a Little Talk with Capital P Poetry, Jim Daniels
Oz, Nancy Eimers
Working in Flour, Jeff Friedman
Scorpio Rising: Selected Poems, Richard Katrovas
The Politics, Benjamin Paloff
Copperhead, Rachel Richardson

2012

Now Make an Altar, Amy Beeder
Still Some Cake, James Cummins
Comet Scar, James Harms
Early Creatures, Native Gods, K. A. Hays

That Was Oasis, Michael McFee
Blue Rust, Joseph Millar
Spitshine, Anne Marie Rooney
Civil Twilight, Margot Schilpp

2013
Oregon, Henry Carlile
Selvage, Donna Johnson
At the Autopsy of Vaslav Nijinksy, Bridget Lowe
Silvertone, Dzvinia Orlowsky
Fibonacci Batman: New & Selected Poems (1991-2011),
        Maureen Seaton
When We Were Cherished, Eve Shelnutt
The Fortunate Era, Arthur Smith
Birds of the Air, David Yezzi

2014
Night Bus to the Afterlife, Peter Cooley
Alexandria, Jasmine Bailey
Dear Gravity, Gregory Djanikian
Pretenders, Jeff Friedman
How I Went Red, Maggie Glover
All That Might Be Done, Samuel Green
Man, Ricardo Pau-Llosa
The Wingless, Cecilia Llompart

2015
The Octopus Game, Nicky Beer
The Voices, Michael Dennis Browne
Domestic Garden, John Hoppenthaler
We Mammals in Hospitable Times, Jynne Dilling Martin
cadabra, Dan Rosenberg
Bartram's Garden, Eleanor Stanford